TRACTION
ENGINES

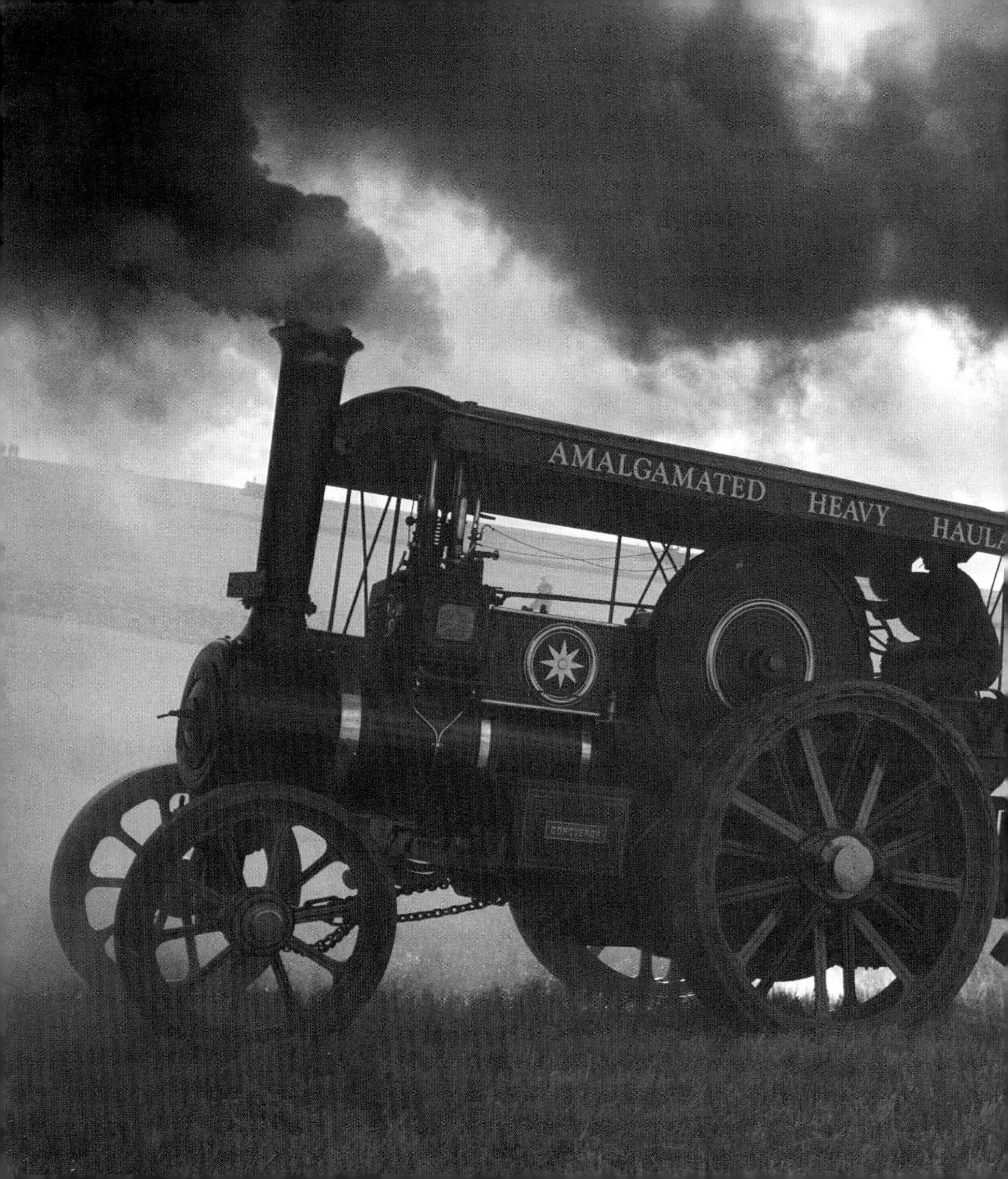
AMALGAMATED HEAVY HAULA

TRACTION ENGINES

ANDREW MORLAND

Osprey Colour Series

Front cover illustration
A steaming 65 hp single-cylinder Case, built in 1916

Back cover illustration
A 110 hp Case, with simple cylinder, ploughing at Rollag, Minnesota

Half-title illustration
A 5 nhp Burrell road locomotive of 1919—Lord Fisher of Lambeth

Title-page illustration
Two Burrells—a 5 nhp and an 8 nhp—lead a 10 nhp Fowler on heavy road train at Stourpaine Bushes in Dorset

About the author

Photojournalist Andrew Morland is an enthusiast of most things mechanical. He owns a small stable of old cars plus several old motorcycles. This is his seventh book in the Osprey Colour Series, although he also contributes to numerous other book and magazine publishers.

Published in 1988 by Osprey Publishing Limited
27A Floral Street, London WC2E 9DP
Member company of the George Philip Group

© Copyright Andrew Morland 1988

British Library Cataloguing in Publication Data

Morland, Andrew
    Traction engines.
    1. Great Britain. Traction engines, to 1986
    2. United States. Traction engines, to 1986
    I. Title
    629.2′292′0941
ISBN 0-85045-805-6

Editor Tony Thacker
Design Norman Brownsword

Filmset by Tameside Filmsetting Limited,
Ashton-under-Lyne, Lancashire
Printed in Hong Kong

Contents

Left
A 5 nhp Burrell road locomotive, seen here in action at Stourpaine Bushes, Dorset

Above
A 45 hp Minneapolis single-tandem compound engine of 1907

Acknowledgements

To begin with, special thanks must go to the organizers and owners of the steam traction engines at the Western Minnesota Steam Threshers Reunion, which takes place at Rollag, Minnesota. This event is held over every Labor Day weekend, lasting a total of four days. Many of the photographs seen here were taken at Rollag, where owners obligingly moved their traction engines, both successfully and unsuccessfully, in the mud for me to take pictures (rather similar to the mud found at Stourpaine Bushes in England!). Janet Briden, the Membership Secretary, is the person to get in touch with regarding information of this event, and can be contacted at P.O. Box 2162, Fargo, North Dakota 58107, USA.

My thanks also go to the North Central Steam & Gas Engine Club of Edgar, Wisconsin, whose annual get-together is held at the end of August, at the farm of Kurt Umnus. In addition, I am grateful to the Ontario Agricultural Museum at Milton, run by the Ontario Ministry of Agriculture & Food, who were kind enough to let me photograph their Sawyer-Massey and Waterloo.

In the UK, I must give particular thanks to the organizers and owners of the traction engines at the biggest steam gathering in the world—Michael Oliver's Great Dorset Steam Fair, held at Stourpaine Bushes. This event, now held during the first week in September, attracts up to 138 restored working traction engines per year. More information can be obtained direct from the Show Office, Dairy Mead, Child Okeford, Blandford Forum, Dorset DT11 8HD.

Other events covered in this book include the Yeovil Festival of Transport, plus those at Stoneleigh, Maidstone and Ham Hill. Held at a picturesque site near Langport in Somerset, the Ham Hill meeting is run by the Somerset Traction Engine Club (Trust) on the third weekend in July each year, and although a small event, it is very large on traction engines.

Special thanks must go to Dr Gerald Parker for his help in captioning the photographs of the Minneapolis Threshing Machine Company's traction engines, and also for his knowledge of the history of this company. Gerald, who is an expert on the Minneapolis steam traction engines, may be contacted at 3420 Birdie Street N.E., Fargo, North Dakota 58102, USA.

All of the historical information about the English traction engines came from Dave Milton, to whom I am very grateful for writing their captions. Dave is an acknowledged steam expert, as well as a well-known commentator at traction engine shows in southern England.

Several other individuals were also very generous with their time and knowledge, namely Pete Loader of Border Engineering Company, the specialists in steam restorations and boiler repairs; Brian Wilkins of Somerset, the owner of *Corn Maiden*, an immaculate 5 nhp Ruston; and Marilyn and Tim at Stillwater, home of the Northwest Thresher Company.

As a guide for those who require further information on steam traction engine events in the USA and Canada, the *Steam and Gas Show Directory* is absolutely essential. This book is printed annually by the Stemgas Publishing Company, P.O. Box 328, Lancaster, Pennsylvania 17603. In the UK, the best source of information on steam shows is the *World Fair Newspaper*, which comes out every Friday—their address is 2 Daltry Street, Oldham OL1 4BB. The National Traction Engine Trust is another invaluable aid to all steam enthusiasts—Mrs Fay Wood, their Membership Secretary, can be contacted at Windrush, Hail Weston, Huntingdon, Cambridgeshire PE19 4JY.

Andrew Morland
Somerset, England 1988

Introduction

A steam engine harnesses the thermal energy of steam to produce mechanical work, i.e. steam from a boiler is expanded to drive a reciprocating piston. The first working drawings of a steam pump and blower appeared in the 1490s, in a technical manuscript by Taccola, or one of his students, at Siena in Italy.

Experimentation in steam power continued over the years until, in 1630, Englishman David Ramsey took out a patent on his steam plough, but it is not known whether this was a portable steam engine or not. However, it took many years for a portable steam engine to be converted to a self-propelling one, because it needed so much more power.

Taking to the water in 1707, Denis Papin from Blois, France, built the first steam-engined boat while exiled in Germany—this boat was propelled by four paddle wheels. Another Frenchman, Joseph Cugnot, from Lorraine, built his 'Fordier' (heavy-load) steam wagon in 1771. This was his third design, and although it could pull 4–5 tons at 12 km/h, the major problem with this machine was that it was impossible to steer.

The single-cylinder engine of a 65 hp Case of 1916

The first really successful steam vehicle was built by Cornishman Richard Trevithick, in 1801. Then, in 1830, Walter Hancock, who owned a bus company, utilized his own design of steam vehicle, running a reliable service in London and the south-east of England, on the terrible cart tracks of the day.

Ransomes of Ipswich, England, built the first traction engine in 1841, with chain drive to the rear axle, and by the late 1850s, in Europe, the traction engine took on its now-standard design, with the firebox at the rear end, centre boiler barrel, smokebox at the front, with the chimney (smoke-stack) at the front on top of the boiler. The drive was from the engine by a train of spur gears to the rear axle, while the steering, using a round steering wheel, was operated by chains from roller worm gear.

The main difference between North American and English traction engines is the lack of a clutch on the English designs. The advantage of the friction clutch is a quicker gearchange; however, its disadvantage is that under full power the clutch can start to slip.

The hp rating was the nominal horsepower quoted, not the actual bhp produced. The nhp was calculated by the area of the piston face, which did not consider rpm, stroke or working pressure. However, it did give an idea of the size of engine; for example, a 6 nhp engine had an 8 in. diameter cylinder, while an 8 nhp engine had a 9 in. diameter cylinder. The Allchin 8 nhp produced 38 bhp, whereas the Savage 8 hp produced 24 bhp. In the UK, nhp ratings were always used, with bhp rates given only for export models, such as the export 10 hp Foster which produced 65 bhp. Generally speaking, the bhp was six times the hp rating. In North America, after 1900, companies started giving bhp figures (though advertised as hp) taken from the flywheel, though in many cases this was exaggerated. The North American engines are classified here as first advertised.

Left
A 110 hp Case traction engine—one of only 18 built

Above
A 45 hp Minneapolis engine (works no. 5761), built in 1907, showing its front water tank, smoke-stack and the single-tandem compound engine

Types of traction engine

General-purpose and agricultural traction engines

This is the most common type of traction engine, being used both for short haulage and as a mobile steam-power engine. On the farm, it could do the threshing, sawing and tree-pulling, plus a great deal more. In the UK, some remained in use until 1950. The single-cylinder was popular for agricultural traction engines, being simple, strong, and with few moving parts, and it could be used by most farm workers with no previous knowledge of machinery. These engines were also used for hauling ploughs in the USA; for example, by 1910, the 110 hp Case simple-cylinder could pull 10 to 12 bottom gang ploughs.

This 24 hp Minneapolis engine (works no. 7804) was built in 1916 and is now owned by Mike Benson of Moorhead, Minnesota. It has a direct-flue boiler, a single cylinder, and a 10 × 11 in. bore and stroke. It was photographed at the Centennial Exposition of the Minneapolis Threshing Machine Company, at Rollag

Ploughing engines, with cable drum

These engines were specially built for operating cable ploughs and were used extensively in Europe and the eastern half of America, the farms of the Midwest being too large for their use. The cable drum is driven by bevel gears, from the engine, with a dog clutch controlled from the driver's platform.

The ploughs normally operated in pairs, one on each side of the field—one engine would pull while the other paid out, the plough being attached to each cable end. They were excellent for deep ploughing, cultivating, mole draining and dredging. The plough engines were

Above
A 12 nhp Fowler ploughing engine of 1916. Note the large drum under the boiler for winching the plough

used and owned by contractors who went around from farm to farm, cultivating up to 40 acres in a day. The pioneer of this ploughing engine was John Fowler, who patented his first special ploughing traction engine in 1856.

11

Road locomotives and showman's traction engines

The road locomotive was designed to haul heavy loads for long journeys on the hard-surfaced roads of the day. In the UK, the motion workings were covered to prevent horses being frightened by the shining moving parts, with the compound engine being used for power and economy. In addition, there was springing off the axles to absorb vibration from the rough road and prevent the working parts of the traction engine becoming loose. The speed gears and belly tanks under the boiler also helped. A load of 60 tons was not unusual, and even 120 tons was possible. Thus, it was not until the 1940s that it became more economical to use the gasoline heavy truck in the UK. However, the lighter road locomotive, operated by one man if under 5 tons, did not last as long as the heavy locomotive, since in the 1930s the gasoline truck was cheaper to run. The lighter loco was used for general haulage, including coal, road stone, timber and furniture.

The showman's locomotive was an adaptation of the road locomotive traction engine. Fitted with dynamos and very highly decorated, it is not surprising that this is now the most collectable machine. The engines were designed to withstand continuous, very heavy usage, having to haul the ever-increasing size of fairground equipment on up to three loaded trailers, sometimes for 100 miles. They also provided the power for the rides, producing the electricity for the fairground, and erected the heavy fairground structures with winch and crane. At the Stourpaine Bushes Steam Fair in England, up to 44 showman's engines can be seen working together, which is a truly impressive sight. However, not all are original—in recent years, many locomotives have been converted to showman's style and, unlike America, the standard locomotive is now rare.

This Fowler 10 nhp showman's road locomotive (works no. 19783), named King Carnival II, *was built in 1932 for Frank McConville of West Hartlepool, Cleveland. It finished its working days cut down to a road-haulage engine, working alongside engine no. 17212 at John Thompson of Wolverhampton, a firm of boilermakers. It has now been restored in preservation to its original form, even down to the lettering on the canopy*

Steam wagons

The inventor of the first steam wagon was Joseph Cugnot, in 1769. Unfortunately, as a result of this invention he was sent to jail in Paris, being considered a danger to the public—every trip he made ended in breakages or explosions, and he even managed to overturn the wagon! It was not until 1802, when Richard Trevithick built his second steam carriage, that people and goods could be carried reliably on smooth roads by a steam wagon.

Two types of compound engines became the norm. The 'overtype' steam wagon used a traction engine locomotive boiler with cylinders on top, while the 'undertype' used a vertical boiler with the engine below and had more carrying space. The problem with the

Here we see the later form of Foden steam wagon on pneumatic tyres, this being works no. 13316, built in 1929. The owners have converted it to a tanker— many Fodens did, in fact, finish their working lives carrying tar tanks. Steam from the engine was used to heat the tar to keep it liquid for spraying on road surfaces

undertype was that dirt and dust were thrown up from the front wheels on to the engine. However, the later undertype high-pressure steam wagon, with enclosed engine and only the rear chain drive exposed, was very fast and reliable. Pneumatic tyres made 60 mph possible.

Road rollers

Thomas Aveling produced the first traction engine with smooth wheels for rolling in 1865. The single-cylinder heavy roller was the most popular and greatly improved the surface of roads for early travellers. The lighter steam rollers for tarmacadam roads, usually 10–12 tons, were worked up to the 1940s.

This Wallis & Steevens 3-ton road roller (Simplicity-type), works no. 7832, was built in 1926 and sold to E. Parry & Company of Putney, London. In 1933 it was sold to W. & J. Glossop of Hipperholme, West Yorkshire. This design was produced primarily for use in the Colonies, where it could use inferior fuels, even wood, and required few skills to drive and maintain

Advance-Rumely

The Advance Thresher Company of Battle Creek, Michigan, was started in 1881. In 1902, this company, together with the Minneapolis Threshing Machine Company, jointly bought the John Abell plant in Ontario and a small factory at Regina, Manitoba, renaming it the American Abell Engine & Thresher Company Limited. This acquisition boosted the sales of Advance steam traction engines into the Canadian prairie market— these traction engines were advertised with the slogan 'Simplicity is Convenience'. The company built simple, single-compound and cross-compound-cylinder engines, ranging from 12–35 hp. During its 23 years of

Right
Eddy Balz from Wausau, Wisconsin, lets the whistle blow on his 22–65 hp Advance-Rumely

Below
A 22–65 hp traction engine, built in 1920, at Kurt Umnus' farm in Edgar, Wisconsin

production, the Advance Thresher Company sold over 12,000 steam traction engines.

In 1911, the Rumely Company of LaPorte, Indiana, bought the Advance Thresher Company of Battle Creek, and also Gaar-Scott & Company of Richmond, Indiana. A year later, the Northwest Thresher Company of Stillwater, Minnesota, was also bought by Rumely. The new company, thus formed, was called the Rumely Products Company and it carried on selling the engines of these manufacturers.

Meinhard and John Rumely had arrived in the USA from Germany in the 1840s and set up a threshing machine business in LaPorte. This company was very successful, and in the mid-1890s it started producing return-flue, single-cylinder steam traction engines that had a rear smoke-stack. As early as 1896, they were selling compound steam engines of 13, 16 and 20 hp. Their main business, though, was selling simple, single-cylinder machines, which were both strong and reliable, to farmers. The largest Rumely built was the 40–140 hp double-cylinder engine.

However, after various economic problems, the firm became known as the Advance-Rumely Company. This company was bought out by the Allis-Chalmers Corporation in 1931.

Main picture
A 22–65 hp traction engine, built in 1919 and owned by Kurt Umnus, being used on Kurt's farm by Ted Knock

Inset left
The dome, whistle, safety valve, governor and flywheel on a 1920 22–65 hp Advance-Rumely

Inset right
The smoke-stack and smokebox on the 22–65 hp engine of 1920

This page & bottom right
Two views of a 120 hp Rumely wood-, coal- and straw-burning engine of 1911, with twin large water tanks on each side of the lagged boiler. This engine is now resident at Rollag

Top left
The factory at LaPorte, Indiana, is depicted in the trademark on this 1904 Rumely 20 hp double-cylinder, rear-mounted steam traction engine

Top right
A 22–65 hp Advance-Rumely of 1920 with a single-cylinder engine. The governor, whistle and oil-pump box are on the left, above the engine

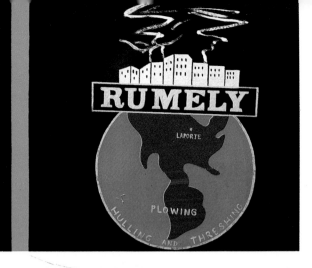

Allchin

Although one of the smaller companies, W. Allchin & Company Limited, situated in Northampton, England, was well known for producing neat engines to 'traditional' designs. The major portion of their engines were single-cylinder, general-purpose types of 7 nhp and 8 nhp.

Right
Built in 1901, Aquarius, a 6 nhp general-purpose engine (works no. 1173), was sold to S. Vousden of Canterbury, Kent, for their agricultural contracting business. The engine finished its working life with the Folkestone & District Water Company, where it was employed for mole draining on the Romney Marshes and for lifting submersible pumps

Below
The Allchin transfer carries the company emblem of the globe, plus basic information concerning the company

Armstrong-Whitworth

Sir W. G. Armstrong-Whitworth Limited of Newcastle upon Tyne, England, was a well-known heavy-engineering company whose products included railway locomotives. During the depression in the early 1920s, they built a series a road rollers as a means of keeping employment up at a time of low order input. However, they did not produce more than 50 engines altogether.

The unusual headstock of this road roller carries the makers' plate and leaves you in no doubt as to the manufacturer

Built in 1923 as one of a batch for stock to overcome a shortage of orders, this 10-ton road roller (works no. 10R2) illustrates the unusual features adopted by this manufacturer—the large cylinder block with piston valves, plate centres not spokes in the rolls, and the unusual colour scheme

Aultman-Taylor

The Aultman-Taylor Machinery Company of Mansfield, Ohio, built nearly 6000 steam traction engines in all. In 1924, however, it was bought by Allis-Chalmers, who built stationary steam engines.

The company was originally formed in 1851 by Cornelius Aultman, under the name of the C. Aultman Company of Canton, Ohio, to make agricultural equipment.

Aultman-Taylor steam engine boilers were of the high-pressure type, with a working pressure of 150 lb. They were famous for their high-pressure, bottom-firebox water boiler, and also the Woolf-patent valve gear, which appeared on the bevel-gear wood and coal boilers. Aultman-Taylor's straw-burner engine used a John Abell-patent boiler, and the boilers were lagged and covered with steel.

Main picture
A 20 hp Aultman-Taylor, built in 1890, seen here heading a procession of traction engines

Inset
A close-up view of the 20 hp Aultman-Taylor engine of 1890

Aveling & Porter

Thomas Aveling was one of the pioneers of traction engine design. His first attempts to produce a self-moving engine were made by converting portables of other firms' manufacture. He designed the first engines in what became the 'conventional' form, and his work on road rolling made Aveling & Porter Limited, based at Rochester in Kent, leaders in roller production.

The company, though, was saved from extinction by the Barford brothers, forming Aveling-Barford Limited, becoming a well-known road roller manufacturer, located at Grantham, Lincolnshire.

This 8-ton tandem road roller, called Murphy *(works no. 12023), was built in 1928 and spent its working life in Ireland. It features a vertical boiler, a small high-speed engine, and power steering*

These two photographs show the boiler of an engine while in the process of restoration. The cylinder block can be seen mounted on its 'saddle', and the tubeplate is ready to be fitted into the front end of the boiler (right)

A 10-ton road roller (works no. 7771), Pegasus was built in 1912 and supplied to Eddisons of Dorchester. These well-known rolling contractors are still in the plant hire business today. The engine was later sold to Surrey County Council, who used it until it was laid aside in 1957. This is the conventional form of road roller for which Aveling & Porter were famous. The company emblem—the prancing horse of Kent—is just visible on the headstock

Built in 1914 as a road-haulage tractor for Kent
County Council, Princess Victoria, a 4 nhp
showman's tractor (works no. 8376), was later sold
to Huntingdon County Council who converted it to a
road roller. Sold on to a private contractor, the
engine finished its days in a Bedfordshire brickyard.
It was converted to its present form in preservation

Avery

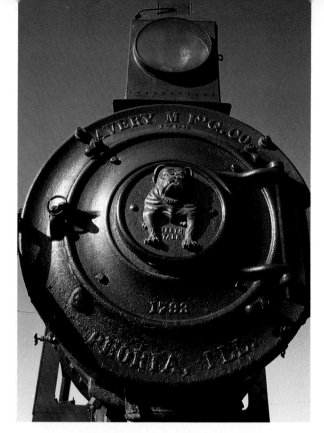

Right
The Avery 'Teeth Talk' trademark in clear view on the smokebox of this 1910 double-cylinder 20 hp traction engine

Below
This 18 hp locomotive-style Avery, built in 1912, with its undermounted double-cylinder engine, was popular for its very smooth performance. However, in dusty and dirty working conditions, the wear on the engine's working parts could be excessive

The Avery brothers manufactured their first steam traction engine at Peoria, Illinois, in 1891. This first Avery was a single-cylinder, straight-flue steam traction engine, with a very strong boiler giving high pressure. (Incidentally, the Avery Company of Peoria had no connection with the tractor company of the same name in Louisville, Kentucky.)

The company became very successful, with many new original ideas that worked well. They had their own reverse gear and clutch, advertised as having 'Great Power, Economical Firing and Strong Hill Climbing'.

However, Avery were best known for their unusual locomotive-style, undermounted, two-cylinder steam tractors of 16, 18, 20, 30, 40 and 50 hp. What was more unusual was their smoothness and quietness compared to a conventional tractor. The main problem with this design, though, was that dirt and dust tended to get into the engine and wear the moving parts. However, the engines were low down so they were easier to work on and clean. For dusty and dirty environments, Avery also had a good range of conventional single-cylinder steam traction engines ranging from 12–50 hp.

At one time, the company was advertised as 'The Largest Tractor Company in the World'. However, even before the depression in the early 1920s, the company was in difficulties. One of the reasons was lack of cash— they were giving too much credit to customers and producing too many different designs of steam engine, with no common use of castings. In addition, the early public failures of their first gas single-cylinder tractors at

Above
This view of the 1912 engine shows the gears on the steering which gave the Avery excellent road manners. These engines were used for road haulage

Below
The 1912 Avery 18 hp locomotive-type cab, with lots of space and a low platform, was popular for crane and steam-shovel use

the Winnipeg Trials, in 1909 and 1910, did not help their image. However, the replacement two- and four-cylinder gas engines were successful.

From 1923 onwards, though, the company died a slow death, suffering many bankruptcies, before finally going under forever in 1941.

Buffalo-Pitts

This strong-sounding name was given to the company started in Buffalo, New York, by twin brothers John and Hiram Pitts, who were involved in making threshing machines. Their first steam traction engines were built in the early 1890s, with rear-facing, simple, single-cylinder engines of 8, 10 and 13 hp. They were compact and light, being very manoeuvrable and of excellent quality. The 10 hp and 13 hp engines came with friction clutch and Woolf-patent reverse gear.

In 1896, their 14, 16, 18 and 20 hp versions, with return-flue straw-burner, had the smoke-stack at the rear of the traction engine next to the driver. These steam engines were well equipped, with Woolf reverse valve gear, Pickering governor, Moore independent steam pump, and Penburtly injector.

Buffalo-Pitts only built single- and double-cylinder simple engines.

The front water tank of a 16 hp engine, built in 1901, with the company logo in view

This 1901 16 hp Buffalo-Pitts, owned by Roger H. Nelson, is known for its quality of construction. The steam engine used a connecting rod forged from one piece of solid steel, with solid ends. The connecting-rod boxes and cross-heads were made of best-quality gun metal, which was unusual for 1901. The double-cylinder, rear-mounted steam engine was centre cranked, with the balance weights just behind the dome above the boiler

Burrell

Charles Burrell & Sons Limited of Thetford, Norfolk, was a family firm noted for retaining traditional methods of production and for producing engines to meet each customer's requirements. It has been said that no two Burrells were ever the same. However, their retention of hand building led to difficulties in the recession of the early 1920s, and Burrells were forced to join with Garretts and others in forming an amalgamated company of agricultural and general engineers. Sadly, even this group could not be saved and it was discontinued in 1932.

A number of engines were built using the single-crank compound system, which was a Burrell patent. It was designed to give the economy of a compound engine, combined with the lower maintenance costs of a single-cylinder type. Burrells were built to a high standard of finish, and this was especially true of their showman's road locomotives.

Right
This 5 nhp road locomotive (works no. 3996), named Conqueror, was built in 1924 and sold to J. H. Henton of Tamworth, Staffordshire. It was used for road haulage and threshing up to 1950, and was then stored under cover. Upon the death of the owner, it was sold into preservation in 1976

Overleaf
Here we have the same engine leading a heavy road train. The use of engines in multiple was a feature of heavy road haulage when very heavy or indivisible loads had to be moved. The other engines involved are a Burrell 8 nhp road locomotive, a 10 nhp Fowler, and another 5 nhp Burrell at the rear of the trailer. Such displays of heavy haulage are a feature of the Great Dorset Steam Fair, held each September near Blandford

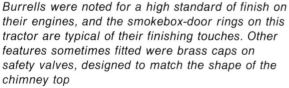

Burrells were noted for a high standard of finish on their engines, and the smokebox-door rings on this tractor are typical of their finishing touches. Other features sometimes fitted were brass caps on safety valves, designed to match the shape of the chimney top

Decorative brasswork abounds on this large showman's road locomotive. The curved brass plate, here giving the makers' name, sometimes carried the name of the owner. The twisted brass covering the canopy supports can be seen and this engine, being named Prince of Wales, carries the Prince of Wales' feathers on the dynamo. The proud owner has added a wonderful collection of lamps

This 7 nhp showman's road locomotive (works no. 3979), called Earl Haig, was built in 1924 and sold to Simonds & Cook, who were West Country amusement caterers. This type of engine would be used to move the fairground equipment from place to place, to assist in erecting the rides by winching trailers and equipment into position, and then to produce electrical power to drive and light the rides. The large dynamo can be seen mounted on the curved extension of the smokebox and is driven by a belt from the flywheel

Main picture

Lord Fisher of Lambeth, *a 5 nhp road locomotive (works no. 3824), was built in 1919 and exhibited at the Royal Dairy Show in London. Purchased by Mr Shire of Thurlbear, near Taunton, Somerset, the engine was used for timber haulage and threshing*

Inset

This 8-ton road roller, named Pride of Somerset *(works no. 4004), was built in 1925 and sold to Messrs Kings of Bishops Lydiard, near Taunton, Somerset. Again we see the high standard of finish on Burrell products. Note the chimney top and the name in brass on the headstock*

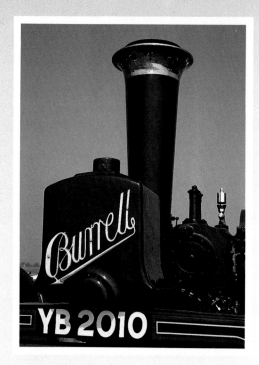

Below

On this 6 nhp showman's road locomotive, the flywheel has been embellished with painted stars. They are designed to match the brass star on the motion cover and, when revolving, produce an interesting effect

Case

The J. I. Case Threshing Machine Company, the internationally best-known manufacturer of early farm equipment and machinery, was started back in 1842 by Jerome Increase Case at Rochester, Wisconsin, when he was only 24 years old. He soon moved to a large rented shop to expand his business in Racine, Wisconsin, the company being known at that time as the Racine Threshing Machine Works. Within three years, he had bought his own shop, where he built all types of agricultural machinery to help save time and effort on the farm—his father was himself a farmer, who had always been keen on new ideas and developments in farming. To get advice and ideas on producing his own

Right
This 80 hp traction engine is ploughing up the car-parking fields outside Rollag, utilizing a working steam pressure of 150 lb per square inch

Below
Here we see the 80 hp Case passing Lake Gunderson at Rollag. This machine has an 11 × 11 in. simple-cylinder engine

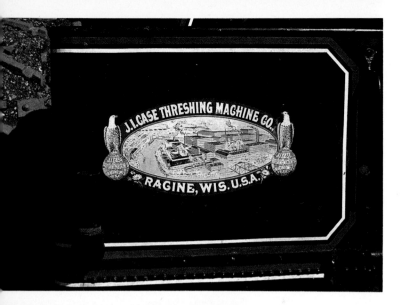

Left
This Case trademark transfer shows the factory on the river at Racine, Wisconsin. Note the ejector hose connection on this 80 hp engine of 1913

thresher that was reliable and yet the most advanced, Jerome worked with farmers on threshing machines. With this background, it was not surprising that Case became the largest manufacturer of threshing machines in the world. In fact, more than 90,000 were built in the years up to 1920. The company also built horsepowers, which were usually a two-horse tread that transmitted the tramping of their feet into belt power for sawmills and threshers.

In 1869, Case sold their first portable steam engine for sawing and threshing. Their first steam traction engine was built in 1876, a total of 75 engines leaving the works that year, and in 1884 the company built their first traction engine with direct-flue boiler and hand steering and differential. This was one of the first USA-produced traction engines, but hand steering and differentials had been used by many English manufacturers as early as 1870.

Just as the company was expanding, Jerome Case died, in 1891. A year later, the Case company experimented with their first internal-combustion tractor. The prototype of this was shown to the public, but the internal-combustion tractor was not in fact produced by Case until 1912, the early carburettor and ignition having proved too unreliable. The steam traction engine proved to be easy to maintain and operate, as well as being economical with good reliability.

The J. I. Case Threshing Machine Company built steam engines of 5 hp up to 150 hp, with simple and compound engines. However, only nine of the large 150 hp engines were ever built. In 1924, the production of steam traction engines finally came to an end, but the company had built an impressive 35,838 units altogether. The Case company did not build any steam cars, but in 1909 it bought out Pierce Racine and built gasoline cars in this factory until 1927. The cars were all with gasoline engines of four or six cylinders, but as they were made to a very high standard, they were not really suitable for the mass market.

Case is now owned by the Tenneco Company, which in 1985 bought the International Harvester Company to become one enormous farm-machinery manufacturer.

Above
The trademark of the Case engines was originally an eagle perched on a branch. In 1894, though, the eagle was placed on top of the world. This cleverly indicated that Case traction engines and farm equipment were being sold all over the world. The idea of the fierce American eagle with folded wings came from the mascot of 'C' Company of the 8th Wisconsin Regiment, called 'Old Abe' (this being Abraham Lincoln's pet name). It is seen here on the smokebox door of a 65 hp engine

Ploughing with a 110 hp Case of 1913 owned by Jim Briden of Fargo, North Dakota, and Norman Pross of Luverne, North Dakota. Note the locomotive-type cab

A 12 gang plough behind the 110 hp Case at Rollag

The 110 hp Case has a 12 × 12 in. simple-cylinder engine. It weighs 18 tons, which is spread over 3 ft wide rear wheels and 16 in. wide front wheels. The rear wheels have a diameter of 7 ft, while the front ones have a diameter of $4\frac{1}{2}$ ft. The 110 hp was ideal for 10 or 12 gang ploughs on the prairie wheat fields

Today's Case logo is split with that of International—on their tractors, the Case name is in front of the International symbol. In 1992, the company will be 150 years old, and many exhibitions are already being planned at shows in America to celebrate this anniversary.

The spinning governor, crank disc, thrusting connecting rod, piston rod and cross-head on a 1916 Case 65 hp traction engine

Here we see a 65 hp Case, built in 1916, working a saw bench at the farm of Kurt Umnus

This 65 hp traction engine is owned by Gary Schacht, a member of the North Central Steam & Gas Engine Club of Edgar, Wisconsin

The 65 hp Case has a simple 10 × 11 in. cylinder

Clayton & Shuttleworth

Early production concentrated on portables, but Clayton & Shuttleworth Limited, based in Lincoln, England, later became known for the production of well-built general-purpose engines and road rollers. In 1924, the company was absorbed by Babcock & Wilcox, who were well-known boiler manufacturers, and a few rollers of Clayton design were produced bearing the Babcock name.

Built in 1923, this 10-ton road roller, called The Thatcher *(works no. 48751), was the first roller of this make to be supplied to W. W. Buncombe of Highbridge, Somerset. Up to that time they had primarily used Aveling & Porter rollers, but they were obviously impressed with it and subsequently bought more Claytons. This roller spent all its working life with this company and was laid aside in the early 1950s. Incidentally, the engine's name refers to its present owner's occupation and does not indicate a political bias!*

Foden

E. Foden, Sons & Company Limited of Sandbach, Cheshire, were noted as manufacturers of steam wagons, but they also produced some very handsome traction engines. Later production concentrated on steam wagons and tractors, but eventually their designs were overtaken by other manufacturers. A change to diesel-engined vehicles kept the company in existence, and they still produce vehicles for heavy haulage and for military use.

This rear wheel belongs to a 6 nhp showman's road locomotive (works no. 2104), named Prospector. *Built in 1910, it was supplied to Shaws, a Lancashire showland family. Note the large number of relatively thin spokes, a Foden feature which gave the wheel a degree of flexibility and improved the riding of the engine*

Above

This steam wagon (works no. 1742), named Queen Mary, *was built in 1908 and supplied to Starkey, Knight & Ford, who were brewers in Tiverton, Devon. The wagon has been restored to its original condition as a brewers' dray and retains its original cast spoke wheels*

Right

Mighty Atom, *a 4 nhp tractor (works no. 14078), was built in 1932 for road haulage. This particular tractor finished its working days hauling fairground loads for Messrs Coles, who were amusement caterers. Many of these tractors were later fitted with rear-mounted winches and used for timber haulage*

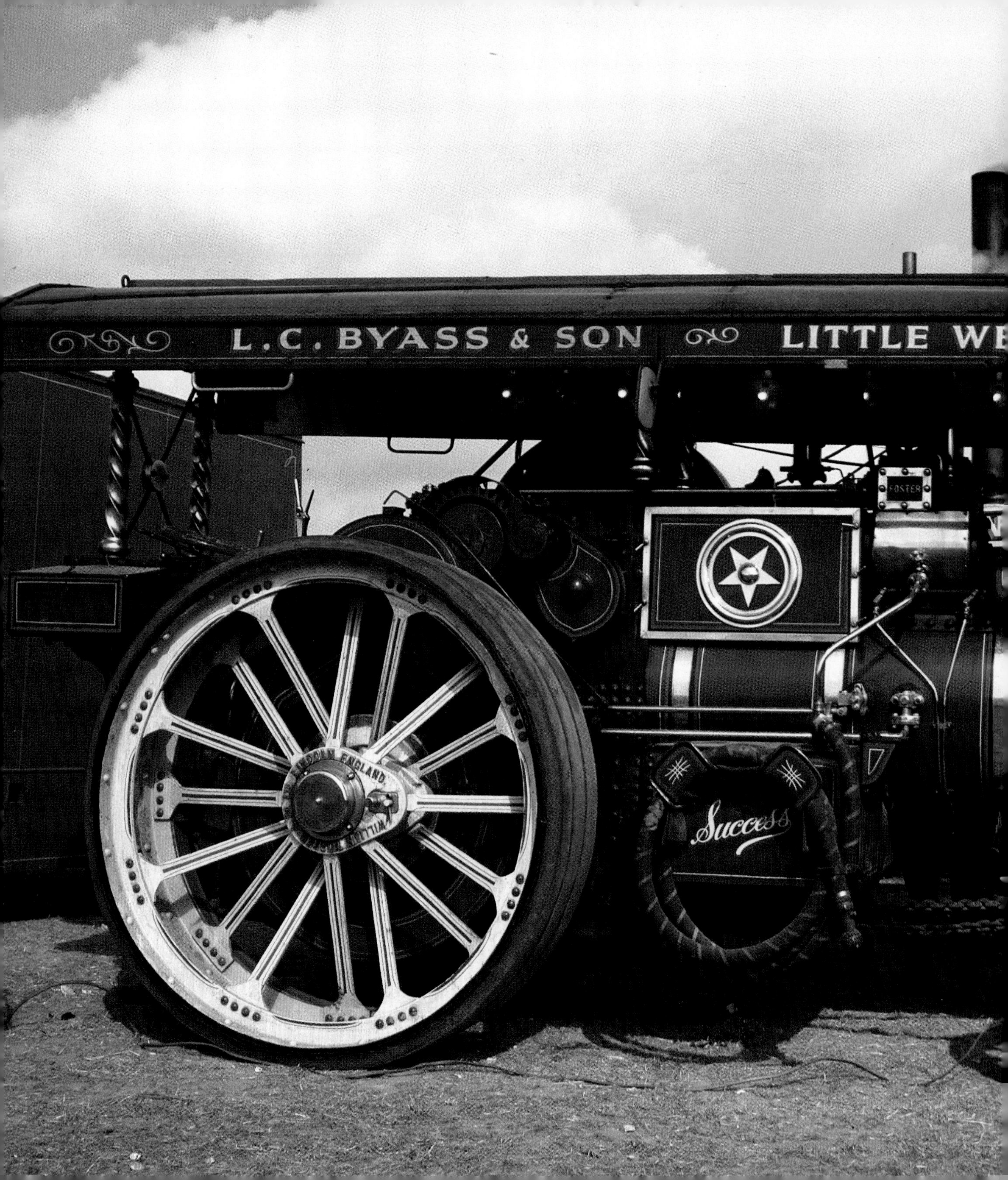
L. C. BYASS & SON
LITTLE WE
FOSTER
Success

Foster

William Foster & Company Limited, based in Lincoln, England, were producers of most forms of traction engines, though they were originally known for their portable engines. During World War 1, they produced the first tanks for the British Army. After the war, this association led to an emblem depicting a tank being included in the decorative ring on the smokebox doors of their engines.

Built in 1934, this 10 nhp showman's road locomotive (works no. 14632), named Success, *was one of the last engines to be constructed for showland use. Owned by Hibble & Mellor, it worked on fairgrounds in the East Midlands. Note that the twisted brass has been chrome-plated to reduce time spent on cleaning*

Right
This 6 nhp general-purpose engine (works no. 12544), called Independence, *was built in 1910 and worked on a farm in Herefordshire, being used for threshing and woodsawing. It is seen here working 'on the belt', probably driving its owner's corn mill*

Below
The company transfer is seen here on the belly tank of a showman's tractor—it is unusual in that it carries a portrait of the firm's founder. The 4 nhp 'Wellington' tractor was a well-designed machine and could be very fast on the road

Fowler

John Fowler & Company (Leeds) Limited was one of the best-known manufacturers of traction engines in the UK. Fowlers were especially noted for the development of ploughing by steam. They developed the two-engine system and sold sets of equipment all over the world. In addition, some very large engines were built and exported for use in sugar-cane production, while their well-known heavy-haulage engines were used by a number of firms for transporting exceptional loads. In many instances, engines would be used in concert to move loads of up to 100 tons.

Built in 1929, this 10 nhp road locomotive (works no. 17212) was supplied to a firm of well-known boilermakers, John Thompson of Wolverhampton. Up to 1948 it was used to transport and erect boilers all over the country. Afterwards, it was used for general work around the company's stockyards

The same engine here forms part of a heavy-haulage road train. Having been built with a crane, the brackets to carry the jib can be seen between the front wheels. The winding drum, mounted in front of the chimney, is shaft driven via gearing on the crankshaft

This 7 nhp general-purpose engine (works no. 12761), named Elsa, was built in 1911. The engine, photographed at a rally in the Midlands in the UK, is finished in an unusual colour scheme. The engine is seen here with its matching living van and trailer, the trailer being used to carry coal and water for the engine while travelling between rallies

Built in 1916, General French, *a 12 nhp Fowler ploughing engine (works no. 14256), finished its working days in Sussex and was then used to block up a hole in a hedge. It was rescued for preservation many years later with trees growing up through it. Here giving a demonstration of steam ploughing, the wire rope can be seen leading away from the large winch drum under the boiler. These engines worked in pairs and the double-ended plough would be winched backwards and forwards across the field while the heavy engines remained on headlands at either side*

Gaar-Scott

John Gaar was the engineer and William Scott was the business man. Together they started Gaar-Scott & Company in Richmond, Indiana, in 1870. The company logo was the face of a tiger, under which was the motto 'Sells and stays sold'.

Gaar-Scott built simple, standard compound and double-tandem compound-cylinder steam traction engines of 13–40 hp. The 'Big Forty', in particular, was a popular ploughing traction engine with its double-tandem compound-cylinder steam engine.

However, the Rumely Company bought out Gaar-Scott & Company in 1911, to form the Rumely Products Company.

A 25 hp double-cylinder engine, built in 1915

Right
A close-up view of the company logo on a 25 hp Gaar-Scott of 1912

Below
The 25 hp single-cylinder traction engine, built in 1912, on parade at Rollag

Garrett

The early production of Richard Garrett & Sons Limited concentrated on portables, and a special workshop was built to produce these using flow-line techniques. In later years, their 4 nhp tractor was a very popular engine, being widely used in light haulage and timber work. Part of the works at Leiston in Suffolk has been preserved and is now a museum of Garrett products.

The Joker is a 4 nhp tractor (Suffolk Punch-type), works no. 33180, which was built in 1919. This engine is the sole survivor of a design produced for direct ploughing—it was intended to compete with the internal-combustion-engined tractors brought over from the USA during World War 1. Although components were made for three such tractors, it is not certain whether the other two were ever assembled

Above
This unconventional tractor has the engine and boiler reversed from normal practice—the smokebox door and chimney are at the rear of this engine. During trials, though, the tractor was found to be too heavy and the design was discontinued

Right
Queen of Great Britain is a 4 nhp showman's tractor (works no. 33486) which was built in 1919 for the War Office. It was later sold to Coles Amusements and was converted for showland use. In this form, it worked around the West Country fairs until 1950 when it was laid up, until purchased for preservation. These smaller versions of the showman's road locomotive were relatively fast on the road and were powerful enough to drive a light ride, such as 'chairoplanes'

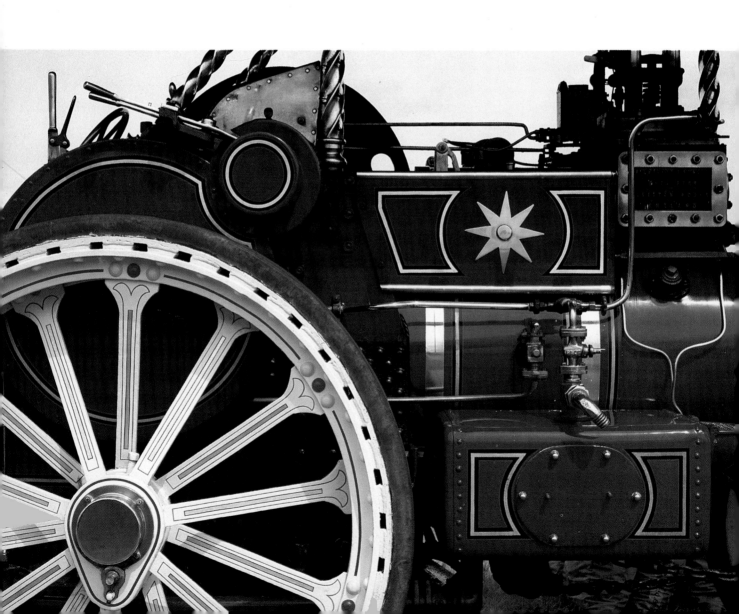

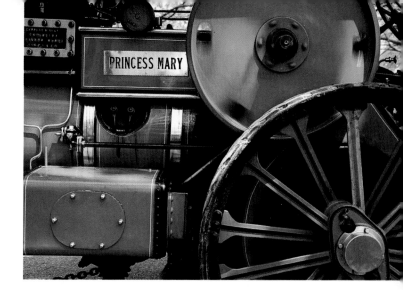

Right

The flywheel side of Princess Mary *(works no. 33278), a tractor built in 1918 for the War Office. The disc-type flywheel which was used on road engines was also used here to avoid frightening horses with the flashing spokes. In addition to the conventional tank beneath the manstand, belly tanks were fitted to give a greater range between stops for water*

Marshall

Together with Aveling & Porter, Marshall Sons & Company Limited of Gainsborough, Lincolnshire, are probably best known for their road rollers. However, they also produced large numbers of traction engines and agricultural machinery of all types. Later production included the distinctive single-cylinder diesel tractor called the 'Field Marshall'.

Hayden Princess *is a 7 nhp general-purpose engine (works no. 36033) which was built in 1901, being sold to George Thurlow of Stowmarket, Suffolk. Subsequently, it had a number of owners before finishing its working life in Sussex. The basic workings of this type of engine are seen here to advantage—the single cylinder, simple motion and the steel straked wheels for grip on wet ground*

Right
The Marshall transfer incorporates the company emblem, Britannia standing on a gear wheel, together with gold medals awarded to their products at various exhibitions

Below
Works no. 84144, this 8-ton road roller (Universal-type) was built in 1928. This design was the Marshall answer to the softer asphalt surfaces. Once again, belly tanks are used to equalize the weight distribution between front and rear rolls. The engine is a small, high-speed unit with the motion enclosed in an oil bath. Note the brass figure of Britannia on the headstock

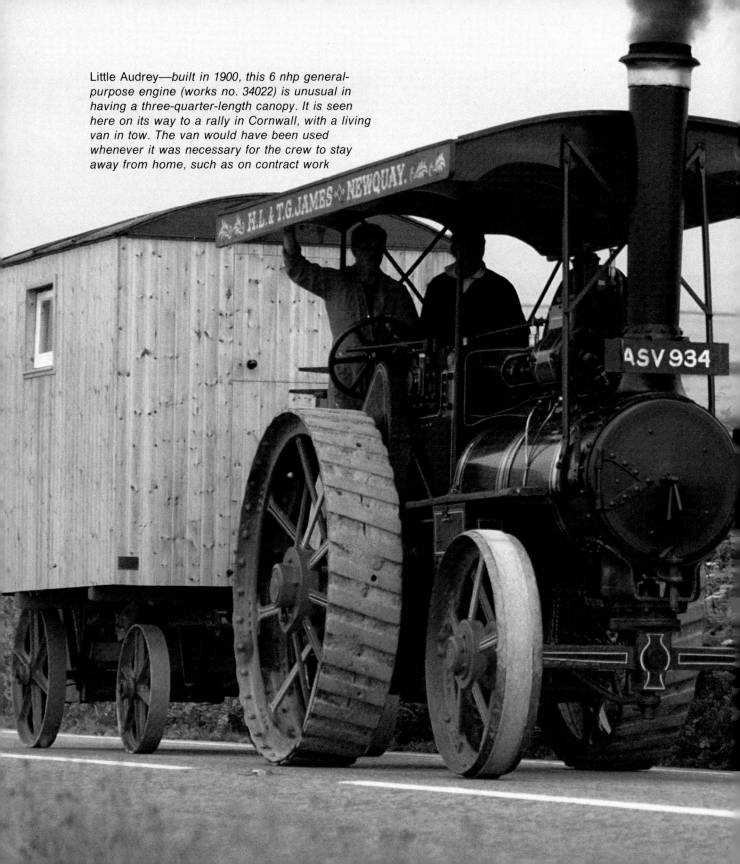

Little Audrey—*built in 1900, this 6 nhp general-purpose engine (works no. 34022) is unusual in having a three-quarter-length canopy. It is seen here on its way to a rally in Cornwall, with a living van in tow. The van would have been used whenever it was necessary for the crew to stay away from home, such as on contract work*

H.L. & T.G. JAMES NEWQUAY.

ASV 934

Inset

Embellishment for a Marshall road locomotive—in this case, Challenger, a 7 nhp loco (works no. 57304) which was built in 1911. Note the inner ring which states 'spring mounted'. General-purpose engines were usually built without springing, but road locomotives which travelled at higher speeds usually had this feature

McLaren

Although the firm of John & Henry McLaren Limited was a near neighbour of John Fowler (located in Leeds), McLarens were a much smaller company. Their products, though, were noted for robustness and simplicity. Particularly well known were their heavy-haulage engines, and a good proportion of their products were exported to Australia and New Zealand. In later years, they built diesel engines for the conversion of Fowler ploughing engines from steam to diesel operation.

Main picture
The Mac is a 6 nhp general-purpose engine (works no. 547) which was built in 1896. This engine worked for a number of owners, ending its working life in Oxfordshire. Here in preservation, it illustrates the robust construction and plain finish of the manufacturer. Black was the standard McLaren finish for this type of engine

Inset
The very distinctive cast chimney base used by McLarens. Plates giving the engine's weight were often fitted to allay the fears of council surveyors who imposed weight restrictions on bridges. However, the plate gave the engine weight as built—when in working order, filled with coal and water, the engine could weigh considerably more

Minneapolis

This engine (works no. 5198) has been owned by Lyle Osten of Callaway, Minnesota, since he was 15 years old, a period of over 30 years. It is the second oldest of the long-boilered, direct-flue engines that are still operating, and is a very unique engine, being the predecessor of a long line of 22 hp engines. There were 536 of these made—it later evolved into the 24 hp when the butt strap boiler was adopted. This engine did a lot of work sawing wood as well as threshing in this area of Minnesota. The bore of the 22 hp is $9\frac{1}{2}$ in., while the stroke is 11 in.

This traction engine (works no. 8453) is owned by the Trosvick brothers of Rothsay, Minnesota, and is a good example of an unrestored 'American' 28 hp machine that is in great shape. Almost everything on this engine is original—it spent most of its career threshing in northwestern Minnesota. The American 28 was brought out in 1917 after 71 'Canadian' 28s had been produced from 1914. The American had a slightly thinner boiler, plus lighter wheels and engine frame—the 28 hp used an 11 in. bore and 11 in. stroke. Engine no. 8453 has been owned by the same family for at least 50 years

The Minneapolis Threshing Machine Company was formed in 1887 by John Stewart McDonald and local businessmen of Minneapolis, with a new factory being built in West Minneapolis, which is now called Hopkins. Ten years earlier, John McDonald had taken over the Fond du Lac Threshing Machine Company in Wisconsin, which meant that there was a lot of capacity available. The new company became the dealer for both Huber of Marion, Ohio, and Upton North Star Steam Traction Engines of Port Huron, Michigan.

In March 1890, the new factory was tooled up and produced its first Minneapolis steam traction engine. Three years later, the company built 395 steam traction engines. Their first direct-flue-boiler and double-cylinder engine, with double smoke-stacks, was produced in 1902. However, the double smoke-stacks were soon changed to a single smoke-stack in production, and many original twins were converted—this was due to the fact that the double stacks hindered the draw on the boiler fire.

In 1904, the direct-flue-boiler, single-cylinder Min-

neapolis engine was built. The 45 hp single-tandem compound engine appeared in 1907, while the following year saw the introduction of the 45 hp double-tandem compound engine. In 1910, the company built its first internal-combustion tractor, called the 'Farm Motor', which was 25 hp. However, by 1913, the return-flue steam traction engine was no longer built, although the 'Canadian'-type 28 hp and 34 hp engines were produced.

Their 20 hp engine was built in 1915 and, like other manufacturers in America at this time, they gave it a bhp rating in advertisements of 22–45 hp.

No steam engines were built in 1918 as the company was tooling up for production of the small 17–30 hp cross-motor, internal-combustion tractor which went on sale in 1919. Their first steel threshing machine appeared in 1922, but production of steam traction engines was small from 1919 until 1924, when the last steam traction engine was produced.

The year 1923 saw a new merged company of the Minneapolis Threshing Machine Company, Hopkins,

and the Minneapolis Steel & Machinery Company, who built the 'Twin City' tractors in Minneapolis. Concentration was fixed on the internal-combustion tractor. At first, the Twin City range of tractors was marketed and in fact sold better than the Minneapolis-Hopkins tractor, but during the following years the Twin City name was slowly dropped in favour of Minneapolis.

In 1929, these two merged companies combined with the Moline Implement Company of Moline, Illinois—Moline had actually stopped production of their tractors in 1923. The new company became known as the Minneapolis-Moline Power Implement Company until 1960, when it was taken over by the White Motor Corporation.

In total, the Minneapolis Threshing Machine Company built 8535 steam engines. This comprised 4345 return-flue-boiler engines of 10–30 hp (with 19 double-cylinder and 26 portable engines), plus 4190 direct-flue-boiler engines of 16–45 hp (with 499 double-cylinder and 3691 single-cylinder engines).

Left

Lee Wyman of Minneapolis, Minnesota, has owned this 20 hp engine (works no. 8702) for two years, and it forms part of the largest private collection of Minneapolis Threshing Machine Company steam traction engines in the USA. It is also the most completely-restored Minneapolis known—in fact, it is in even better condition than when it was released from the factory, being now equipped with the Baker balanced valve. This engine, which uses a $9\frac{1}{4}$ in. bore and 11 in. stroke, was featured in the 1924 Minneapolis Threshing Machine Company catalogue—this company made more 20 hp traction engines than any other model, totalling 977 units

Below

Gerald Parker has owned this Minneapolis traction engine (works no. 8692) for six years. From the information he has managed to acquire, it seems to have spent very little time working anywhere, having endured very little wear. It did do some threshing and sawmill work in central North Dakota, but sat under cover for most of the years from 1924 onwards doing nothing. It is equipped with the Baker balanced valve and has a very good boiler

Inset

Owned by Nick Blatti, this 18 hp traction engine was built in 1903 (works no. 4086), with a direct-flue boiler and double cylinder, having a 6 × 10 in. bore and stroke. This engine is one of only 35 built of 18 hp

Main picture
The Nick Blatti-owned double-cylinder 18 hp Minneapolis with its single smoke-stack. It originally had the famous double smoke-stack, but like most was converted by the Minneapolis Threshing Machine Company to a single stack. Here it is photographed next to a 353 railroad engine which is taking on water at Rollag

Norman Pross of Luverne, North Dakota, owns this traction engine (works no. 5761), which is of the single-tandem-compound design, being one of only seven engines made to this design by Minneapolis. The company developed the big 45 hp in 1907 and only built it in that year. In 1908 they came out with the 45 hp double-tandem-compound design, which used the same boiler as the single 45 and the single 35s. This engine was pieced together from parts found all over this area of the USA and Canada. It took three years to assemble, most of that time being spent 'full-time' by one man who worked in a large machine shop in Fargo, North Dakota. Many parts were not available and had to be either built up from scratch or borrowed from a 35 hp engine and a 45 hp double-tandem-compound one, also located in North Dakota (these engines have not been restored and do not run). The boiler was completely rebuilt and was tested using ultrasonic thickness gauges, and all the welding plus the longitudinal seam were X-rayed for defects. It is one of the most unique engines in existence today in the USA. The high-pressure cylinder is $10\frac{1}{4}$ in. bore, while the low-pressure cylinder is 15 in. bore and the stroke 12 in.—this is a very large cylinder! Norman had owned the engine parts and the boiler for about 30 years before restoration took place

Nichols & Shepard

From a blacksmith's shop in Battle Creek, Michigan, in 1848, John Nichols, with financial help from David Shepard, started an agricultural equipment and small stationary steam engine business.

They sold their first steam traction engine in 1887. Although Nichols died in 1891, and Shepard in 1904, the company continued to flourish until 1929, when it was taken over by the Oliver Farm Equipment Company. Today, Olivers is still in business as part of the White Motor Corporation, which also has Minneapolis-Moline under its wing.

Nichols & Shepard traction engines were well known for their strongly constructed boilers, advertised as the thickest boiler plate in the traction engine business. They made simple, single- and double-cylinder steam engines from 8 hp to the 120 hp of 1910, and also compound engines of 13–26 hp.

The company logo as seen on the front of a 100-gallon water tank

*Belting up the flywheel for the saw bench. Note the
wooden shoes on the friction clutch*

Seen working at the saw bench at Kurt Umnus' farm is a 20–70 hp Nichols & Shepard engine burning wood. It can also burn coal or straw

Port Huron

In 1882, the Upton-Port Huron Company built their first traction engine. Eight years later, in 1890, the company became the Port Huron Company, building the famous Port Huron-Woolf compound engine in 1896. The Huron valve gear was more precise than that of other engines of the time and boasted a four per cent saving in fuel. Their economy engine, which had 9 ft long boiler tubes, was known as the 'Longfellow' traction engine. These traction engines were advertised as the most economical engines in the world. The company made double- and single-cylinder Longfellows, as well as standard simple-cylinder, compound and double-compound engines, totalling approximately 8600 units.

Main picture
The Port Huron compound-cylinder steam traction engine was popular for heavy ploughing and heavy haulage, being powerful yet economical. This 24 hp engine, built in 1915, is owned by Bob Brekken, seen here at the Rollag parade

Inset
The 24 hp front-mounted compound-cylinder engine, built in 1915. The cast smokebox is full of information for enthusiasts

Ransomes, Sims & Jefferies

Ransomes, Sims & Jefferies Limited is a firm of general and agricultural engineers who built traction engines as part of their range of equipment. The company is still in existence (situated at Ipswich, Suffolk) and has been known to borrow a preserved engine to display on their stand at shows and exhibitions.

This 7 nhp general-purpose engine (works no. 26995), named Mendip Lady, *was built in 1916 and spent its working life in Huntingdon, Cambridgeshire, on general agricultural contracting duties. It is a fine example of the basic single-cylinder traction engine. Such machines were easy to use and relatively simple to maintain*

Above
Some manufacturers used transfers to embellish their engines. Here the makers use them to show the gold medals obtained by their products at various exhibitions

Right
The cylinder is the powerhouse of the engine, and here the manufacturer's plate giving the works number can be seen on the valve-chest cover. The red box is the mechanical lubricator feeding oil to the cylinder

Reeves

A 1906 Reeves 25 hp double-simple-cylinder engine at work, powering the sawmill next to a nice Dodge pick-up at the Western Minnesota Steam Threshers Reunion. In the 1930s, this engine was used to power the sawmill at Park Rapids-Menagha, Minnesota

The Reeves Company of Columbus, Indiana, was formed in 1874, their first engine being a double-cylinder, rear-mounted traction engine.

Reeves made many simple, double- and cross-compound steam engines, besides a wide range of agricultural equipment. Their steam engines were always technically sound and made to a high standard with good ideas. Most had jacketed boilers, to save energy, plus some enclosure of the gearing and engine to reduce wear from dust and dirt. The Reeves cross-compound engine of 1903, with its high- and low-pressure cylinders, similar to Burrell's, was very successful. With its lower boiler pressure, the boiler lasted longer yet had more power with less fuel. A good selling point for doubters of this advanced design was that, in case of an emergency, the engine could be instantly converted into a simple, double-cylinder one, with both cylinders using live steam from the boiler. This also gave almost unlimited power for an extra-heavy load.

Despite the success of the Reeves traction engines, Emerson-Brantingham bought out the company in 1912. By 1925, however, Emerson-Brantingham had closed the Reeves factory, although the old factory at Columbus was used by a local bank to start a new company, the Cummins Engine Company.

This 1906 25 hp Reeves is owned by Myron Danielson of Rothsay, Minnesota, seen here at Rollag. This engine was also used for road building in the 1930s

Robey

Robey & Company Limited, of Lincoln, England, are best remembered for the production of some unusual designs of road rollers and for their high-speed road-haulage tractor. Together with their steam wagons, these engines incorporated an unusual design of boiler and a small, high-speed engine unit. Incidentally, a Robey tri-tandem roller spent the last months of its working life helping to build a section of the M1 motorway.

Main picture
Wally is a 7 nhp general-purpose engine (works no. 29333) which was built in 1910 and sold to Mr Wright of Blockley, Gloucestershire. It was later sold to James Blackwell of North Leach, Gloucestershire, and used for threshing up to 1948. Afterwards, it was sold for scrap and left to rot until purchased for preservation in 1969 with many parts missing. The engine is named after its last driver

Inset
The makers obviously intended their engine to be an advertisement for their products, with not only the transfer but a large cast plate on the valve-chest cover as well. The device on top of the cylinder block with the pulley and round weights is the governor. This is used to control the speed of the engine as the load fluctuates when working 'on the belt'

Russell

The partnership of Charles and Clement Russell with Charles Nahum, Sen., led to the formation of C. M. Russell & Company. The Russell family had come from Scotland to New England, before moving to Massillon, Ohio, in 1838. The company itself was started in Massillon in 1842, manufacturing railroad cars and steam shovels. Later on, boxcars, passenger cars, dump wagons and small steam engines were built— steam traction engines were only a small part of their business.

Their traction engines were built simple for ease of maintenance, and engines of 6–150 hp with simple and compound cylinders were produced. The company, though, like many others of the time, got into difficulties in 1927 and was sold at auction. The new company did not build traction engines, but it did service them until it, too, went out of business in 1942.

Main picture
This early 1920s Russell was rated at 90 belt hp, or 30 hp standard. It is a simple-cylinder engine of 10 × 13 in., photographed here at Rollag

Inset
The front-mounted cylinder on this 1924 30–90 hp Russell has a double-ported valve, which was patented by Giddings

Ruston

This company went through a series of changes, starting as Ruston Proctor & Company Limited. At a time when they were well known for portables, they became Ruston Limited. In 1918, they joined forces with Richard Hornsby & Sons Limited to form Ruston & Hornsby Limited. This company went on to manufacture excavators and is still in existence today, making diesel engines in Lincoln, England.

The clean lines of the basic general-purpose engine are seen to advantage here. Note the footboard mounted off the boiler to give the driver easy access for oiling the motion

This is Corn Maiden, *a 5 nhp general-purpose
engine (works no. 52266) which was built in 1918 for
the British War Office but was never used by them.
It was sold in 1920 at a sale in Slough to Charles
James of Pen-y-Parc, Herefordshire, and was used
by him for threshing up to 1952*

Here we see the engine demonstrating the sort of job it was asked to do during its working life. Such demonstrations of threshing, woodsawing, etc, are often included in the events at traction engine rallies. Great care is needed to position the engine with its flywheel exactly in line with the pulley on the threshing drum

Sawyer-Massey

John Fisher produced his first threshing machine in 1836 and, with his cousin Calvin McQuesten's injection of money, the company prospered. In the 1840s, C. D. Sawyer, also a relative, joined the firm with his two brothers. When John Fisher died, though, the business was renamed D. Sawyer & Company.

They were building portable steam engines by the 1860s, and in 1887 they became import agents for Aveling & Porter road rollers from England. Soon afterwards, the company brought out their 13 hp, simple, single-cylinder traction engine. From the 1890s onwards, traction engines of 18, 20, 22, 25 and 35 hp were being produced; after 1900, 68 and 76 hp engines were also being built for the prairie farms.

In 1892, H. A. Massey bought a 40 per cent share in the firm, and the name was changed to Sawyer-Massey & Company Limited. This company, based at Hamilton, Ontario, became the biggest manufacturer of agricultural steam engines worldwide. In 1910, however, the Massey family withdrew their interest in Sawyer. The reason for this was never given, but steam enthusiasts say the Massey family objected to a policy decision by the Sawyer company to increase production of steam engines. But this contradicts what actually happened in 1910, when Sawyer-Massey started production of some very successful gas tractors. So who knows the real reason?

The 1918 76 hp Sawyer-Massey owned by the Ontario Ministry of Agriculture & Food, on show at the Milton Museum, Ontario

*Another view of the 76 hp Sawyer-Massey traction
engine, built in 1918*

Sentinel

Starting life in Glasgow, this company moved to Shropshire to acquire room for expansion, becoming Sentinel (Shrewsbury) Limited in the process. Their production comprised steam wagons and railway shunting locomotives, and they were the main competitor of Foden. In the 1930s, their last design, the 'S' type, was far ahead of other wagons of that period, but Sentinel were also forced into the production of diesel-engined vehicles. Later on, the company became part of Rolls-Royce and specialized in the manufacture of diesel engines.

This steam wagon (S4-type), works no. 8843, was built in 1933 as a tipping wagon. It was later laid aside and used for spares to keep other wagons running. It has now been restored as a timber tractor using the engine from a Sentinel shunting locomotive to power the rear-mounted winch

The Sentinel S4 design was far ahead of others of its time, and this view shows the very clean lines to the front of the cab. Note the electric lights and the boiler mounted behind the crew. Coal is carried in a hopper in the cab roof, being gravity-fed into the boiler

"Sentinel"

S4 Timber Tractor 1933

GOOLD BROS.
CAMERTON · BATH

UJ 2112

Wallis & Steevens

Wallis & Steevens Limited of Basingstoke, Hampshire, were probably best known for their later designs of road roller—the 'Advance' and the 'Simplicity'. Their traction engines employed their patent 'expansion' valve gear which was designed to give economy when driving equipment on the belt. The company went on to produce diesel road rollers, still using the name 'Advance'.

Hampshire Rambler—*built in 1910, this 7 nhp general-purpose engine (works no. 7115) spent its working life in Hampshire. It finally went into preservation with a great character of the steam world, 'Boxer' Old of Braishfield, near Romsey, and new owners have since restored the engine's original name,* Boxer's Beauty

Above

This 10-ton road roller (Advance-type), named Little
Wonder *(works no. 7878), was built in 1926, being
purchased by Torquay Borough Council with whom
it spent its working life. This type of roller was
designed to work with the softer asphalt materials.
By carrying the water in belly tanks, either side of
the boiler, the weight was more equally distributed
between front and rear rolls*

Right

Pride of the Hills *was built in 1936 and sold to
Hampshire County Council. This 8-ton road roller
(Advance-type), works no. 8100, differs from* Little
Wonder *in having full-width belly tanks. An absence
of covers enables the motion to be seen, and it will
be noticed that there is no flywheel. This, together
with the use of twin cylinders, enables the roller to
reverse quickly without leaving indentations in the
softer asphalt surfaces. In addition, the roller has
quite a turn of speed and is seen here 'assisting'
the heavy-haulage gang*

Waterloo

The Waterloo Manufacturing Company was started in 1850, in Waterloo, Ontario, by Jacob Bricker, producing agricultural tools and implements. In 1888, the wealthy Snider family bought into the Waterloo company and were able, with their capital, to take over the Haggard Bros. Foundry at Brampton. There they built their first traction engine. This 14 hp engine was side mounted, the boiler being supported on springs. The single cylinder was front mounted above the smokebox, at the bottom of the pretty diamond-topped smoke-stack. The later engines of 14, 16, 18 and 20 hp were centre cranked.

The last Waterloo steam traction engine was built in 1925, when the company was bought out by McKay of Australia. Today, the company survives as distributors of 'Belle City' threshers and Minneapolis-Moline farm tractors.

The front-mounted, centre-cranked 16 hp Waterloo engine of 1892, photographed at the Ontario Agricultural Museum at Milton, Ontario, where the engine is on show. The rear of the boiler is mounted on a large cast frame below massive bull gears

*The threshing machinery of the Waterloo
Manufacturing Company had been sold as the Lion
Brand from the 1850s onwards—thus the smokebox
door of this 16 hp engine of 1892 has the smiling
lion's head on it*